Illustrated
Stories *from the* Bible

Volume 4

AUTHORS
George and Marilyn Durrant
Former Professor of Ancient Scriptures

Educational Doctorate

ARTIST AND ART DIRECTOR
Vernon Murdock
Artist Illustrator

Bachelor of Fine Arts
Graduate Work, University of Madrid,
*   Spain*

CORRELATORS AND DIRECTORS
Steven R. Shallenberger, *President*
Community Press, Wisdom House, Eagle
*   Marketing Corporation*

Bachelor of Science; Accounting, Business.
SCMP, Graduate School of Business, Harvard
*   University.*

Paul R. Cheesman
Director of Scripture in Religious Study Center
Chaplain, U.S. Navy

Doctor of Religious Education

Lael J. Woodbury
Chairman, National Committee on Royalties,
*   American Theatre Association*

Doctorate of Theater, University of Illinois

ADVISORS
Dale T. Tingey
Director American Indian Services and
*   Research Center*

Doctor of Philosophy, Guidance and
*   Counseling; Washington State University*

Reverend Raymond E. Ansel
Ordained Minister

Southwestern Assemblies of God College, Texas
*   Berean Bible School, Missouri*

Millie Foster Cheesman
Writer, Poetess

M.J. Bardon
Missionary-Pastor, Grace Baptist Church

Th. M. Clarksville School of Theology
*   Clarksville, Tennessee*

Reverend William R. Schroeder
United Church of Christ

United Theological Seminary of the Twin Cities
*   New Brighton, Minnesota*

SECOND EDITION VOLUME 4, 1981

Lithographed in U.S.A.
by
COMMUNITY PRESS, INC.
P.O. Box 1229
Antioch, California 94509

A Member of
The American Bookseller's Association
New York, New York

Moreover as for me, God forbid that I should sin against the LORD in ceasing to pray for you: but I will teach you the good and the right way:

Only fear the LORD, and serve him in truth with all your heart: for consider how great things he hath done for you.

But if ye shall still do wickedly, ye shall be consumed, both ye and your king.

1 Samuel 12:23-25

Smilax: a climbing plant found in the Holy Land. It has broad shiny evergreen leaves, small greenish-yellow flowers, and red berries. The young shoots are eaten like asparagus.

Dedicated to boys and girls throughout the world and to all who love the Bible.

A nondenominational work.

CONTENTS

Our story so far..7

A New Hope in Israel *(Samson Is Born)*..8

Having Your Own Way Is the Wrong Way *(Samson's Selfishness)* 15

You Must Do Your Part if Promises Are to Come True *(Samson's Exciting Life)*............20

Strength Alone Is Not Enough *(The Gates of Gaza)* 27

Evil Can Do What Armies Cannot Do *(Samson and Delilah)* 34

One of the Bible's Happiest Stories *(The Story of Ruth)* 48

Loaned to the Lord *(Samuel's Boyhood)* 60

Listen When The Lord Calls *(The Lord Speaks to Samuel)* 67

Do Not Make Fun of Sacred Things *(Losing the Ark of the Covenant)* 74

A Foolish Desire *(The Israelites Want a King)* 81

Not an Accidental Meeting *(Samuel Chooses Saul to be King)* 85

Things Will Work Out if We Obey God *(Saul Becomes King)* 92

Obedience Is the Only Way *(Saul's Disobedience)* 94

The Lord Knows Us When We Are Young *(David Chosen by Samuel)* 101

The Faith to Win *(David and Goliath)*...110

Preview of Volume Five 135

Our story so far . . .

Volumes One, Two, and Three have helped us understand God's mighty creation of the earth, the story of our first parents—Adam and Eve, the faith of Noah as he built the great ark, and the foolish people who tried to build a tower to heaven. We also became acquainted with Abraham, Isaac, and Jacob. Joseph's story inspired us to be faithful.

Moses and the Israelites then spent forty difficult years in the desert wilderness. God sent them manna, a special food from heaven. Snakes came into their camp, but God gave them a way to learn obedience and to live, even when bitten by these poisonous serpents.

Remember the donkey that was able to speak? That was a humorous and inspiring story. However, we were saddened when God's great prophet Moses said goodbye to the people he loved so dearly.

Joshua, the new leader, was a man of faith and courage. He led his people across the Jordan River. Then came the amazing story of the crumbling of the walls of Jericho. After many battles the Israelites were finally able to conquer most of the people in the Promised Land, their homeland.

God blessed his people greatly but, instead of worshipping him as they should have, they began to worship false gods. Because of this they became a weak people and enemy armies conquered them. Then came Deborah, a woman prophetess, who inspired Israel to do better. Next, Gideon, a humble farmer, defeated an enemy army with just a few brave men.

As exciting and inspiring as these first three volumes have been, this fourth volume is even more so. We will be thrilled as we read of big, brave, but foolish Samson; beautiful Ruth; the mighty prophet Samuel; the first happy and then sad King Saul; and finally one of the Bible's most beloved heroes, David.

Volume Four does indeed teach us much about God and his love for his children.

A NEW HOPE IN ISRAEL
Judges Chapters 1-13

Many years had passed since the death of the mighty leader Joshua. Deborah, the woman who inspired the Israelites, had also died. Gideon too was gone. Then for a time a man named Jephthah had led Israel to victories over the Canaanites, but he also had grown old and died. Forty years had passed with no great leaders and the Israelites were no longer a strong and mighty nation as they had been in Joshua's day. It was at this time that a good man named Manoah lived.

Manoah and his wife felt much sorrow in their hearts for two reasons: First, they longed for freedom but instead were slaves to the Philistines. Second, they had hoped and prayed for a child for many years, yet they were still childless.

Imagine the joy and excitement that came to Manoah and his wife when, in answer to their prayers, an angel came from heaven and told them ". . . thou shalt conceive, and bear a son; . . . and he shall begin to deliver Israel out of the hand of the Philistines." (Judges 13:5)

The angel also told them that their son was to be "a Nazarite unto God." This meant that the child would grow up to be a special servant of the Lord, and as such he should not drink wine or strong drink or cut his hair. Manoah and his wife were thrilled. Manoah was so happy he almost shouted, "We will be free! We will be free!" His wife added, "Yes, and we shall have a son of our own to hold and to love."

Because of the good news the faithful couple built an altar to God to show him how thankful they were that their prayers were soon to be answered.

After some months the cry of a newborn child was heard in Israel. This infant, born to Manoah and his wife, would someday become the mighty Samson. Surely he would save Israel from their enemies.

Jerusalem Meadow Saffron
(Autumn Crocus)

HAVING YOUR OWN WAY IS THE WRONG WAY
Judges Chapter 14

We know nothing of Samson's boyhood days. We can imagine he played games with the other boys and that his team seldom if ever lost. Those watching him play may have said to Samson's parents: "You must be proud of him. He is so skillful and strong."

Samson was an unusual boy in many ways, but sometimes being outstanding can cause problems. In Samson's case that is exactly what happened. Both his body and his will were strong. Perhaps his parents wondered about him: "He seems selfish and will not do as we tell him." Then, remembering the promise of the angel, they would feel better as they thought: "But someday he will be a leader and help deliver us from our enemy. God has promised us that."

15

God had promised that Samson would be a leader, but God works through his people on earth. If his promises are to come true, the people who receive the promise must do their part. Samson cared little about rules or obedience and he often got into trouble because he used his great strength unwisely. Years went by. When he had grown to the age of a young man, Samson rebelled against his parents by demanding, "I have seen a woman in Timnath of the daughters of the Philistines: now therefore get her for me to wife." (Judges 14:2)

His parents were very upset and frantically tried to talk him out of his desire by saying, "*Is there* never a woman among the daughters of thy brethren [our people] . . . ?" They were worried because God had commanded the Israelites to marry among their own people. Samson did not honor his parents. He cared only about his own desires and he quickly replied, "Get her for me; for she pleaseth me well." (Judges 14:3)

The parents were brokenhearted at their son's attitude. Yet there was still hope. After all, God had promised that Samson would help deliver Israel out of the cruel hands of the Philistines. Surely that promise would still come true.

Others of the tribe of Dan, which was Samson's tribe, knew of God's promise that this strong young man would someday help save them. They hoped that promise would come true for they were desperate in their desire to be a free people. They must have been bitterly disappointed as they saw this fun-loving, selfish young man do one foolish thing after another. "Why can't he think of us?" they must have asked. "All he seems to care about is himself." Samson didn't care what they thought. It was his life and he would live it his way.

YOU MUST DO YOUR PART IF PROMISES ARE TO COME TRUE
Judges Chapters 14, 15

One day after Samson had grown to his full and incredible strength, he walked down a lonely road. Suddenly a young lion leaped into his path and roared at him. This foolish lion had picked a fight with the wrong man. Samson, with no weapon except his two bare hands, quickly killed the poor beast.

Just think what a man with such strength could have done if he had only been obedient to his parents and to God and if he had had a greater desire to help his people.

If only someone today could shout way back into history and say, "Samson, grow up! Change your ways. Lead your people into battle and free them from the Philistines." But he could not have heard anyone from the present, nor would he even listen to the people of his own time.

Days, months, and years passed as Samson continued his selfish and rebellious life. Somehow he could not find the time for his true mission in life. What a sad story.

However, there were times when he did give the Philistines problems, but he always did it in his own impulsive way. For example, one day he lost a bet to some Philistines. In order to pay them the thirty suits of clothes he owed them, he went among a group of Philistine men and killed thirty of them. He then took their clothes and gave these stolen things to those who had won the bet. Such foolish behavior brought him fame but was disappointing to those who loved him.

On another occasion he returned to his wife, after running off for some time, and discovered her father had given her to a Philistine. This made him so angry that he caught three hundred foxes and tied them together tail to tail. Then he fastened a torch to them and turned them loose in the dried cornfields of the Philistines.

As can be imagined, fires were soon burning everywhere. Samson's anger probably turned to laughter as he stood on a hill and watched the flames, the confusion, and the excitement caused by his actions. The Philistines did not laugh though and were determined to get even. Samson's behavior would only make things worse instead of better for the Israelites.

STRENGTH ALONE IS NOT ENOUGH
Judges Chapters 15, 16

When his own people heard the news of the fires in the cornfields, they probably chuckled and said, "He is quite a man and he sure gave them what they deserved. But when will he settle down and lead us against the Philistines as the angel promised that he would?"

After the fires had burned out, Samson returned to a place near his home. The angry Philistines were not far behind. They demanded that this troublemaking vandal be turned over to them. Samson loved an exciting challenge and, not wanting the Philistines to harm his people, he willingly allowed his friends to bind his hands with ropes. He then departed with the angry Philistines.

As they traveled along the road, some Philistines shouted insults at him. Their words made him so angry that he flexed his strong muscles and snapped the cords like string. "And he found a new jawbone of . . . [a donkey], and put forth his hand, and took it, and slew a thousand men therewith." (Judges 15:15)

What a man! What a hero! If only he could have been as strong on the inside as he was on the outside. God had given him physical strength but it was up to Samson to build his own inward strength. Tragically that was something he could not seem to do.

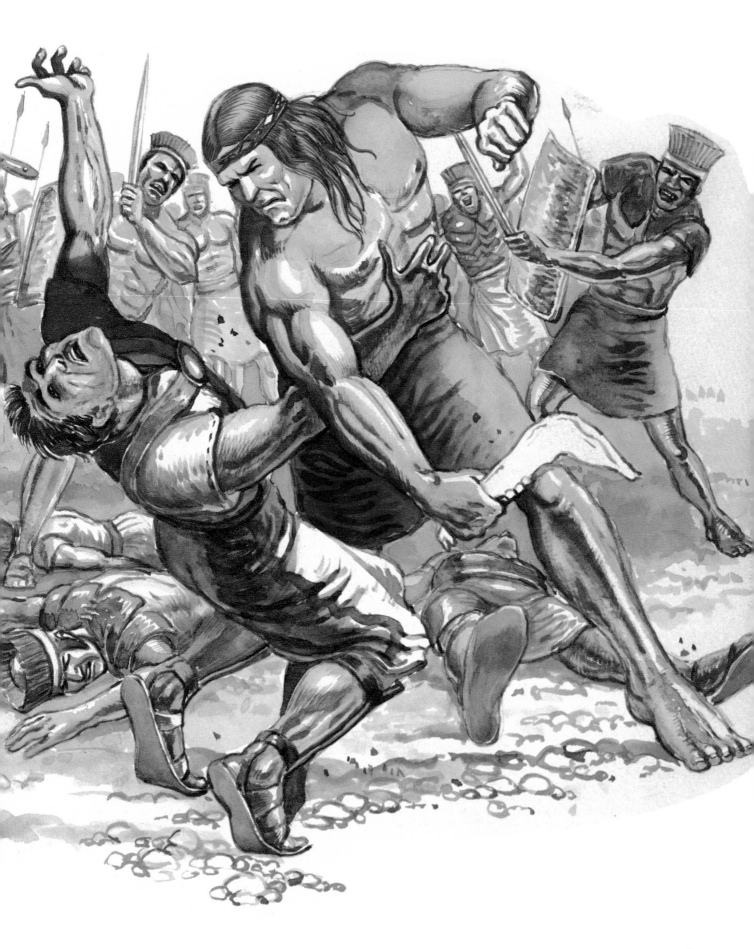

But God continued to love and bless him. In many ways this fun-loving, betting, fighting, strong man had a good heart. For twenty years Samson did lead the Israelites, although apparently with little success. The Philistines were still the masters and the Israelites were still a weak and conquered people.

As time went by, Samson journeyed to a city called Gaza. The Philistines, still trying to capture him, learned that he was within their walled city. Excitedly they locked the huge gate. Now they had him, or at least they thought they did! They knew that he was strong but they didn't know how strong. At midnight Samson quietly prepared to leave the city, but to his surprise he found the gate locked.

He paused and stared at the high walls and the massive gate. A smile crossed his face as he thought of the Philistines, who undoubtedly imagined they had captured him at last. Then he ran forward, ripped off the doors of the gate, put them on his back, and carried them to the top of the hill.

When light of morning came, one can picture the surprise of those who thought they had captured him. Where were the doors to the gate? How could they have gotten on top of the hill outside the city? Could Samson have done that? How could such a strong man ever be captured? Was there a way? Someone quietly spoke, "I know how we might get him. Ten thousand men can't beat him, but perhaps one woman can." Soon a plan was devised. A plan that would be the downfall of the world's strongest man.

EVIL CAN DO WHAT ARMIES CANNOT DO
Judges Chapter 16

Samson "loved a woman in the valley of Sorek, whose name *was* Delilah." (Judges 16:4) By her outward appearance Delilah was truly beautiful; however, she was not to be trusted. The Philistine leaders saw an opportunity to conquer Samson through Delilah. They offered her much silver if she would find the secret of Samson's great strength and how he might be overcome.

Knowing that Samson loved her, Delilah asked him, "Tell me, I pray thee, wherein thy great strength lieth. . . ." (Judges 16:6) Fun-loving Samson jokingly told her, "If they bind me with seven green withs [willowy, supple twigs] that were never dried, then shall I be weak, and be as another man." (Judges 16:7) After telling her this, the two of them talked about other things until Samson became tired and went to sleep.

Distaff Thistle

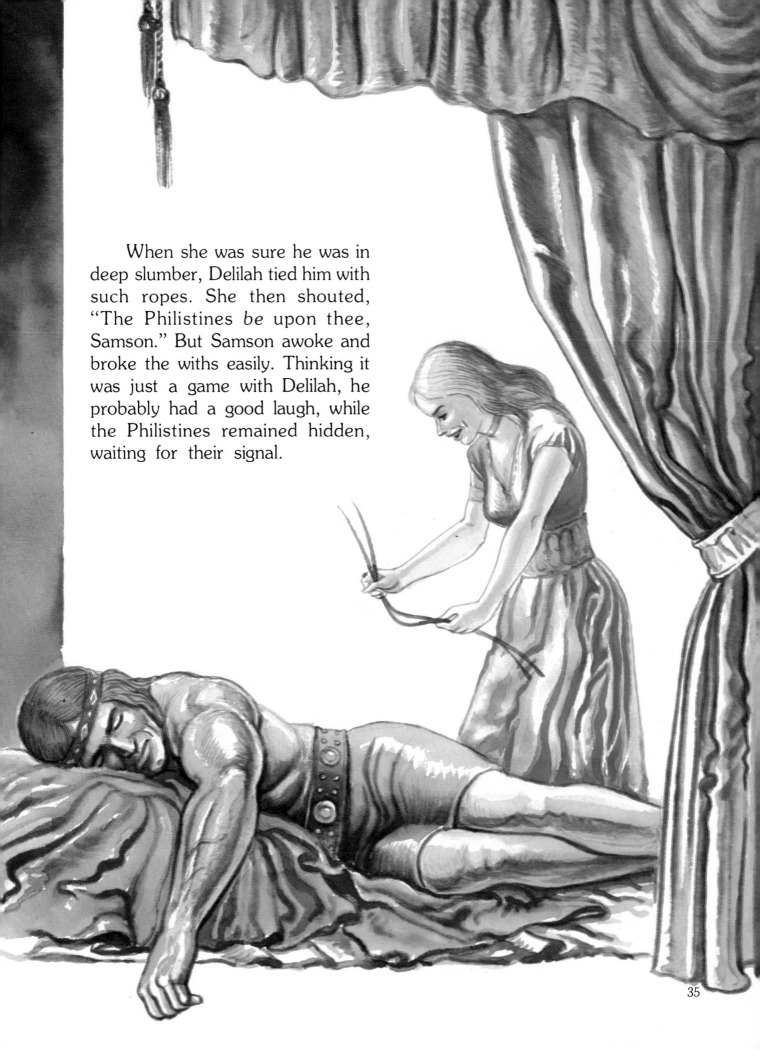

When she was sure he was in deep slumber, Delilah tied him with such ropes. She then shouted, "The Philistines *be* upon thee, Samson." But Samson awoke and broke the withs easily. Thinking it was just a game with Delilah, he probably had a good laugh, while the Philistines remained hidden, waiting for their signal.

Delilah was not pleased with what had happened. She told Samson that he had mocked her and she begged him to tell her the truth about his great strength.

Samson told her, in a voice that seemed sincere, to tie him this time ". . . with new ropes that never were occupied." After he had fallen asleep, Delilah followed instructions but again Samson broke the ropes. This time Delilah was beside herself with anger.

Samson was enjoying this entire experience. To him it was nothing more than a big joke. He continued his tricks by telling her next to braid his hair. To her displeasure that did not work either.

Delilah cried and said, "How canst thou say, I love thee . . . and hast not told me wherein thy great strength *lieth*." (Judges 16:15)

Delilah pleaded with Samson each day to reveal his secret. Using poor judgment because of his wicked ways, he finally weakened and told her the truth. He said, "There hath not come a razor upon mine head; for I *have been* a Nazarite unto God . . . if I be shaven, then my strength will go from me, and I shall become weak, and be like any *other* man." (Judges 16:17)

That night Samson slept soundly. Delilah called for a man and caused him to shave off Samson's hair while he slept. As Samson's hair fell, the hope of Israel fell with it. Satan had won. By lies and insincere love a wicked woman had done what an army could not do. Weak Samson was soon carried away by the enemy soldiers.

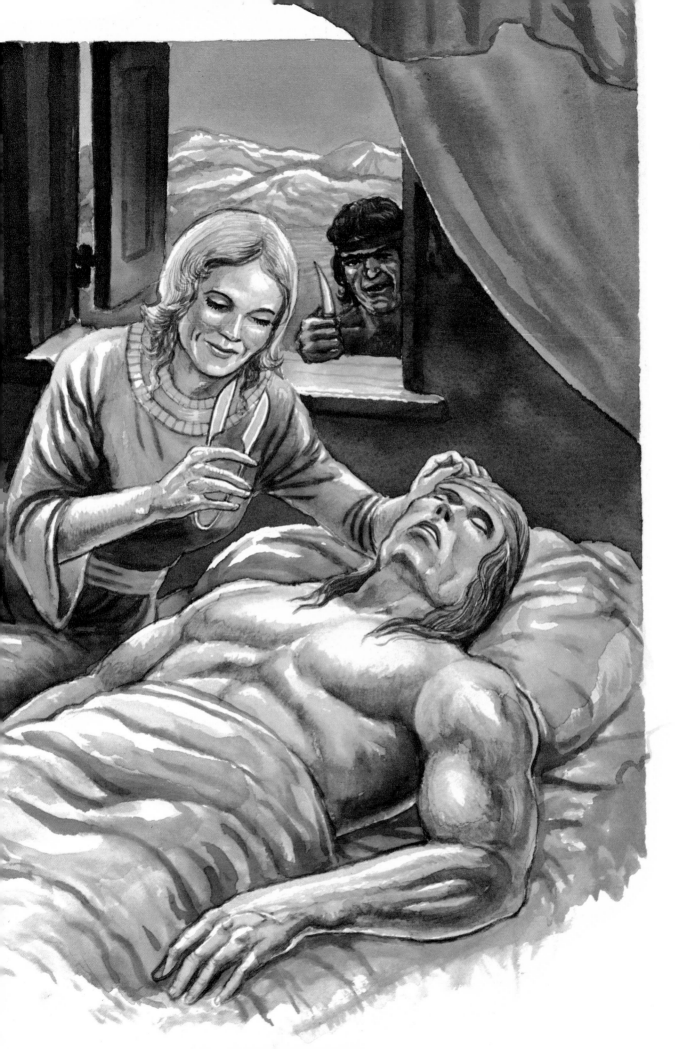

Samson's eyes were burned out and he was placed in a Philistine prison ". . . and bound with fetters [shackles] of brass; and he did grind in the prison house." (Judges 16:21) In other words, they used him as an animal to push the grinding stones around and around in a circle. Time passed and, as his hair began to grow, his strength began to return.

Finally, the Philistines held a great celebration to mock Samson, and he was brought out of the prison into the large banquet room. As they laughed and made fun of him, he asked the lad who had brought him into the room to guide him to the pillars that held up the building in order that he might lean on them. Then, praying to God, he asked for strength. "And Samson took hold of

the two middle pillars upon which the house stood, and on which it was borne up, of the one with his right hand, and of the other with his left. . . . And he bowed himself with *all his* might; and the house fell. . . ." (Judges 16:29, 30) Thus he killed many of his enemies, but also himself."

Samson was dead, but his memory will never die. He is loved today because in many ways he was a hero. His failure is a disappointment because he could have been one of God's great and noble leaders. Instead, because he did everything his own way, he is one of history's most infamous failures. The choice had been his.

THINK ABOUT IT

1. Do you know anyone who is somewhat like Samson?
2. Is there a bit of Samson in you? Why?
3. What could Samson have done differently?
4. How can you make sure your life is better spent than Samson's?

ONE OF THE BIBLE'S
HAPPIEST STORIES
The Book of Ruth

The story of Samson was an exciting and adventurous kind of story which ended in sorrow. The story of Ruth is just the opposite. Her story is a quiet and beautiful love story.

Ruth wondered about the handsome young stranger who stood in the market-place. He was with another young man and an older woman who apparently was their mother. A friend told her that these three strangers were Israelites who had come to Moab to escape a famine in Israel. The father had come with them but had died. The family was now living in Ruth's village.

49

Ruth, a young Moabite maiden, felt drawn to these people. They became friends, and in time she fell in love with and married the son Mahlon. Mahlon and his family taught Ruth about the God of Israel, and she became a faithful follower of the Lord.

Chilion, the other son, also married a Moabite girl and the family lived happily in their new land. Then both young husbands became ill and died. After a period of mourning, Naomi called her daughters-in-law to her. She told them of her plans to return to her home in Israel and suggested that they return to the homes of their parents in Moab. She explained, "You will be better off if you stay here. This is your land. In Israel you will be strangers and you will not feel at home."

Orpah, the wife of Chilion, agreed with this advice and returned to the home of her parents. But Ruth did not feel the same way. She said, "Intreat me not [please don't ask me] to leave thee, *or* to return from following after thee: for whither thou goest, I will go; and where thou lodgest, I will lodge: thy people *shall be* my people, and thy God my God." (Ruth 1:16)

The mother Naomi was deeply touched by this beautiful appeal. She was glad to have her beloved daughter-in-law return with her to Israel.

After the long journey back to Israel Naomi and Ruth established a new home in Bethlehem. Ruth worked as a gleaner in the grainfields, gathering the kernels of grain that fell to the ground when the men harvested the fields. A man named Boaz saw Ruth in the field and asked his servant, "Who is she?" The servant answered, "It *is* the Moabitish damsel [girl] that came back with Naomi out of the country of Moab." (Ruth 2:6)

Boaz went to Ruth and told her to glean only in his fields and not to work elsewhere. He promised her that none of his men would touch her and she could have drinking water from the vessels provided by his men. She asked, "Why do you treat me so well when I am a stranger?" He replied, ". . . [I know] all that thou hast done unto thy mother in law since the death of thine husband: and *how* thou hast left thy father and thy mother . . . and art come unto a people which thou knewest not heretofore [before]." (Ruth 2:11)

As Boaz thought about Ruth and got to know her better, he fell in love with her. He knew that she had been good to Naomi and that she loved the Lord. It was also clear to him that she would be a choice wife. He desired with all his heart to marry her. Ruth loved Boaz also and wanted to be his wife.

Soon all the customs and laws of Israel had been obeyed and these two faithful people were married. They started married life with a hope that they would have a wonderful family. Their prayers were answered, for after a time they had a fine son whom they named Obed. As the years passed they had a grandson named Jesse and finally a great-grandson named David. It was this David who became a mighty king in Israel.

They knew, as did all the Israelites, that someday a Savior would be born who would break the bonds of death and allow everyone to be resurrected and live again. In their fondest dreams they may have even hoped that this Savior, who was to be Jesus Christ, would someday be born through their family line.

Ruth's life testifies that if a person loves God and obeys his words, he or she will experience much happiness. Of course, Ruth had days of sadness (such as when her first husband died), but through all of her problems she remained faithful and became one of the most beloved women in the Bible.

THINK ABOUT IT

1. The Bible says Naomi and her family went to Moab to escape a famine, but what do you think was the real reason the Lord had them go to Moab?
2. Why did Boaz fall in love with Ruth?
3. How does Ruth's life show us that God knows what the future will bring?

LOANED TO THE LORD
1 Samuel Chapter 1

Would a person always recognize the Lord's voice when he speaks? The Bible gives an account of a person who heard the Lord speak but didn't know who it was. That person was a boy named Samuel.

Before Samuel was born, Hannah, who was to be his mother, went to the tabernacle to pray. She had wanted a child for many years but none had been born to her.

As she prayed with all her heart, she moved her lips without actually saying the words out loud. The old prophet Eli, who was passing by, thought she was drunk at first and rebuked her. She explained to him that she was not drunk but desired a child and was praying that God would bless her. Eli understood and comforted her by saying, "Go in peace: and the God of Israel grant *thee* thy petition that thou hast asked of him." (1 Samuel 1:17) Hannah was thrilled with the prophet's words because she knew that when a prophet speaks, his words will come true. Now she knew she would have a child.

Hannah promised the Lord that if he would bless her with a son, she would raise him until he was able to care for himself and then she would take him to the prophet Eli at the tabernacle. Thereafter he could work for the Lord for the rest of his life. Months later this faithful woman did indeed have a son, whom she named Samuel.

As she had promised, she cared for him until he was old enough to care for himself. Then she packed his clothes, took young Samuel to the prophet Eli, and said, "For this child I prayed; and the LORD hath given me my petition which I asked of him: Therefore also I have lent him to the LORD; as long as he liveth he shall be lent to the LORD." (1 Samuel 1:27, 28) It must have been very hard for Hannah to give her only child to the service of the Lord.

Thus did Hannah keep her promise to the Lord. After Samuel went to live with Eli, the Lord blessed Hannah and her husband with other sons and daughters.

Any person can receive happiness by lending his or her talents to help the Lord. The Lord does his work through his children on earth and he especially needs the help of those who will keep their promises.

THINK ABOUT IT

1. What are some ways you can "lend yourself" to the Lord?
2. How does the story of Samuel show us that we can help the Lord even while we are young?

LISTEN WHEN THE LORD CALLS
1 Samuel Chapters 2, 3

Samuel's new home was not a happy one. Eli had two sons who were unwilling to do as their father asked and were a bad example to the people. Eli was glad to have young Samuel around for he could see that, unlike his own sons, this boy helped rather than hindered the work of the Lord.

Not long after he came to live with Eli, Samuel had a remarkable experience. As he lay awake in his bed one night, he heard the Lord call out his name, "Samuel." Samuel, thinking the voice was that of Eli, who was sleeping nearby, said, "Here *am* I." He quickly ran to the old prophet and asked what he desired. Eli replied, "I called not; lie down again." (1 Samuel 3:5)

A few minutes later the Lord again called, "Samuel." Again the boy ran to the prophet and again he was told, "I didn't call you. Go back to bed."

Having just laid himself down, Samuel again heard his name and went to Eli for the third time. By this time Eli was beginning to wonder. He said, "Go, lie down: and it shall be, if he call thee, that thou shalt say, Speak, LORD; for thy servant heareth." (1 Samuel 3:9)

Samuel did as he was told and this time when the Lord spoke, he replied, "Speak; for thy servant heareth." The Lord said, "Behold, I will do a thing in Israel, at which both the ears of every one that heareth it shall tingle." (1 Samuel 3:10, 11)

The Lord then told Samuel that because Eli had allowed his sons to be disobedient, this man and his family would experience great sadness in the future. The next morning Eli, knowing of the Lord's visit, wanted to know what the Lord had said. Samuel felt badly about the message but told Eli the full story. Eli sadly replied, "It *is* the LORD: let him do what seemeth him good." (1 Samuel 3:18)

"And Samuel grew, and the LORD was with him. . . ." (1 Samuel 3:19) Because of the way he lived, everyone in Israel knew that Samuel was a true prophet.

THINK ABOUT IT

The Lord's voice is often soft and sometimes only comes as a thought in our hearts. When he speaks to us, what should our answer be?

DO NOT MAKE FUN OF SACRED THINGS
1 Samuel Chapters 4-6

Samuel did his best to lead the Israelites to victory over the Philistines, but victory was not easy. Once, in order to help the army, the sacred ark of the covenant was brought out from the tabernacle to the battlefield. Because of the unfaithfulness of the people the ark was

captured by the Philistines. Sadness swept over all Israel when they learned the ark was gone. Eli died of shock when he heard the ark had been taken and that his two sons had been killed in battle. As the Lord had told Samuel years before, the people's ears truly did tingle when they heard of this great sadness.

The wicked Philistines were delighted to have the sacred ark. In order to mock Israel's God, they placed the ark before the statue of their pagan god Dagon. Their mocking soon changed to fear, however.

During the night the statue of Dagon fell on its face in the dirt. They set it in place again, and the next morning found it broken into pieces on the ground. Frantically they moved the ark of the covenant from one city to another and each time great destruction came to that city.

Finally they said, ". . . Send away the ark of the God of Israel, and let it go again to his own place. . . ." (1 Samuel 5:11) So a cart was made and the ark was placed on it along with some gold. Two milk cows were harnessed and, amidst the rejoicing of the Israelites, the cows pulled the ark home. Thus God showed his great love for his people and once again made the fact very clear that, as he had covenanted or promised Abraham, Isaac, Jacob, Joseph, Moses, and Joshua, he would indeed be with the Israelites.

If they would be true to him, he would make them a
blessed people among all other peoples in the world.

A FOOLISH DESIRE
1 Samuel Chapters 7, 8

Samuel had great power given to him by the Lord. During one battle, as the Israelites were losing, Samuel came and prayed for his army and offered a sacrifice to God. As the enemy was about to attack, ". . . the LORD thundered with a great thunder on that day upon the Philistines . . . and they were smitten before Israel." (1 Samuel 7:10) We can see that the Lord can speak quietly, as he did to the boy Samuel, or loudly, as he did that day on the battlefront. Whatever is needed at the moment, the Lord can and will do if people have faith.

Years went by and, under the leadership of the prophet, the Israelites completely defeated the Philistines. The Israelites were once again free, as they had been in the days of Joshua. "And Samuel judged [led] Israel all the days of his life." (1 Samuel 7:15)

Eli's sons had been disobedient and had caused their father much sorrow. Now Samuel was alarmed and saddened to see his own sons behaving the same way. He knew that after his death they would not be worthy to become Israel's leaders.

About this same time Samuel could not believe what he was hearing from the people. Everywhere he went they shouted, "Give us a king!"

Samuel was greatly discouraged. He had tried to be a good leader, but he felt rejected now that the people wanted a king. In sadness he prayed. The Lord replied, ". . . they have not rejected thee, but they have rejected me, that I should not reign over them." (1 Samuel 8:7) The people knew that Samuel spoke for God. Thus they had indeed, by rejecting the prophet, rejected God.

The people continued to shout, "We don't want a prophet to lead us. We want a king like other great nations have." Samuel replied, "If you have a king, he will take your sons into the army, collect taxes, and make your daughters his servants." Samuel gave other reasons why having a king was not a good idea, but the people did not listen and repeated, "Give us a king!" The Lord spoke to Samuel and said, "Hearken unto their voice, and make them a king." (1 Samuel 8:22)

THINK ABOUT IT

1. Why did the people want a king?
2. Do we sometimes desire things that are not for the best?
3. Will the Lord let us have our way? Why?

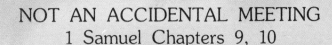

NOT AN ACCIDENTAL MEETING
1 Samuel Chapters 9, 10

We have read about some large men in the Bible—some were even giants. One man who was very large, although not quite a giant, was to become the first king of Israel. His name was Saul.

Following the Lord's request, Samuel spent much of his time searching for a man who would be a suitable king. The meeting of Saul and Samuel was not an accidental meeting because God never works by accident in any matters. Although he allows people to choose right or wrong, he always acts and directs with a purpose.

Just prior to their meeting Saul was out looking for some lost cattle that belonged to his father. After searching in many parts of the land, his discouraged group was about ready to return home. At this time he learned that Samuel was in a nearby city and he decided to go ask the prophet how to find his cattle. Little did Saul know how important this decision was.

"Now the LORD had told Samuel . . . [the day before], To morrow about this time I will send thee a man out of the land of Benjamin, and thou shalt anoint him *to be* captain [king] over my people Israel. . . ." (1 Samuel 9:15, 16)

The next day when Samuel saw Saul, the Lord said unto Samuel, "Behold the man whom I spake to thee of! . . ." (1 Samuel 9:17)

Samuel told Saul not to worry about the cattle for they had already been found. Saul and his men ate with Samuel and spent the night. The next day Samuel sent the others ahead and walked alone with Saul.

After talking for some time, the two stopped by the side of the road, No one was near. "THEN Samuel took a vial of oil, and poured *it* upon his [Saul's] head. . . ." (1 Samuel 10:1)

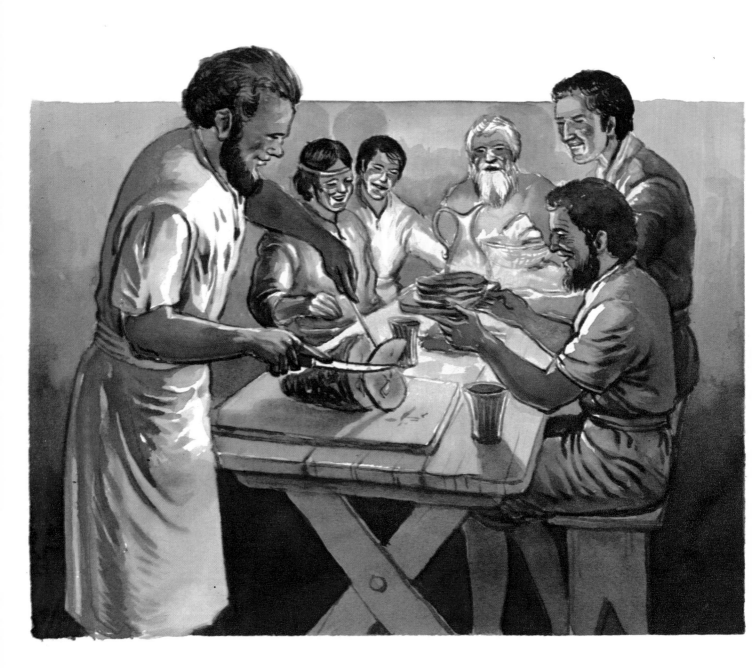

As Samuel explained the matter to him, Saul was astonished to know that God had chosen him to be the future king of Israel. Samuel comforted the fearful Saul by saying, "And the Spirit of the LORD will come upon thee, and thou . . . shalt be turned into another man." (1 Samuel 10:6)

When Saul and Samuel were through talking, Saul turned to leave. At that time ". . . God gave him another heart. . . ." Saul now knew that the Lord would not ask him to do anything unless he also made it possible for him to do it. Saul was ". . . a choice young man . . . and *there was* not among the children of Israel a goodlier person that he: from his shoulders and upward *he was* higher than any of the people." (1 Samuel 10:9; 9:2)

Saul, who was then unknown to almost all of Israel, had met the prophet of God. Soon all Israel would know Saul. With his new heart and as a new man, Saul departed for home. He would never be the same again.

THINK ABOUT IT

1. What does the scripture mean when it says, "God gave him another heart"?
2. Whenever we hear the voice of God and obey, what will God do for us?

THINGS WILL WORK OUT IF WE OBEY GOD
1 Samuel Chapter 10

A meeting was called and many Israelites came. Samuel spoke to those present and announced, "Saul will be our new king." The people began to look for the man named Saul, but even those who knew him could not see him. Saul was hiding. Soon someone discovered him and brought him forth. As Saul stood before the multitude, "he was higher than any of the people from his shoulders and upward." When the people saw him they shouted, "God save the king!"

Samuel the prophet then gave a speech to his beloved people. He reminded them of his own life and how he had tried to serve them without ever being a burden to them. He reviewed the works of other great prophets such as Moses, Aaron, and Jacob. He went on to tell them, "You have chosen a new kind of leader. You now have a king instead of a prophet." He concluded by warning them that things would go well for them if they obeyed God, but if they forgot God they would have many hard, sad times ahead. The people listened carefully to the prophet and knew that he spoke the truth. Some perhaps wondered, "What will the future bring?" Others must have realized that only time would tell.

93

OBEDIENCE IS THE ONLY WAY
1 Samuel Chapter 15

Saul was a humble yet strong king. He was determined to do things just the right way, but no matter how hard he tried he still made mistakes. It was good that Samuel was nearby to help him out. On one occasion, when Saul and his army were leaving for a battle against the Amalekites, Samuel said to Saul, "When you have won the battle, be certain to destroy *all* the people of that nation and also all their animals." Saul listened carefully and agreed to do exactly as the prophet said. The two said goodbye and Saul and his army marched away.

Sometime later a great battle was fought and the Israelites completely defeated their enemy. Their king was captured, but Saul decided not to kill him. Also, some of the sheep and oxen were of such good stock that Saul may have thought, "These are such beautiful animals. It would be foolish to destroy them." Saul somehow put out of his mind what Samuel had told him and his promise to Samuel. He must have ordered something like, "Round them up. We will take them back to Israel."

As the army was journeying homeward, the Lord told Samuel of Saul's disobedience. Samuel prayed all night about the matter and the next day went out to meet the army. As Samuel and Saul met, Saul was the first to speak, saying, ". . . I have performed the commandment of the LORD.

"And Samuel said, What *meaneth* then this bleating of the sheep in mine ears . . . ?" (1 Samuel 15:13, 14) Saul's quick reply was, "I brought them home to offer them as sacrifices unto the Lord."

Samuel was angry and sternly rebuked Saul by saying, "The Lord anointed you king over Israel and sent you to completely destroy the Amalekites, but you did things your own way."

97

Saul could tell that Samuel was displeased, so he quickly began to make excuses. "I utterly destroyed the Amalekites, except for King Agag, and the people brought the animals home to offer them as a sacrifice." Samuel's firm voice replied with the power of a prophet, ". . . Behold, to obey *is* better than sacrifice. . . ." (1 Samuel 15:22)

Saul had no answer for he knew he had done the wrong thing.

Samuel then added, ". . . thou hast rejected the word of the LORD, and the LORD hath rejected thee from being king over Israel." (1 Samuel 15:26)

Saul listened carefully to this heartbreaking news that came from the prophet's lips. He was told he was no longer worthy to be king and that a new king would soon be chosen. Sadly Saul turned away and departed.

Because Saul had disobeyed God, he had started on a path that would lead him further and further away from God. From then on his life would become filled with sorrow, hate, and misery.

THINK ABOUT IT

1. When the Lord speaks, we are free to obey or disobey. If we disobey, what usually happens?
2. Did Saul really have a new heart when he first became king? Why did he fail?

THE LORD KNOWS US WHEN WE ARE YOUNG
1 Samuel Chapter 16

The Lord now told Samuel to find another person to become king. This search would be quite different from the first one and would lead to a much different man than had been found before. This time the Lord sent Samuel to Bethlehem to the house of a man named Jesse.

Following a long journey, the gray-haired prophet arrived at the place he had been told to go. After entering, he asked to meet each of Jesse's sons. The father sent word to his sons and one by one they came and stood before the prophet.

Each son was outstanding. First came Eliab. When Samuel saw him he was impressed and said to himself, "Surely the LORD's anointed *is* before him." (1 Samuel 16:6)

At that time the Lord said something that should never be forgotten. He said, "Look not on his countenance, or on the height of his stature; because I have refused him: for *the LORD seeth* not as man

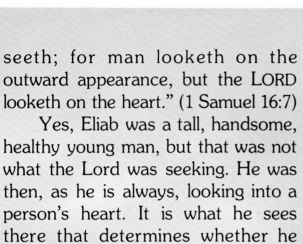

seeth; for man looketh on the outward appearance, but the LORD looketh on the heart." (1 Samuel 16:7)

Yes, Eliab was a tall, handsome, healthy young man, but that was not what the Lord was seeking. He was then, as he is always, looking into a person's heart. It is what he sees there that determines whether he can use that person to be his servant.

The next son to stand before the prophet was Abinadab. Again Samuel saw a fine-looking man, but again the Lord said, "No."

Shammah was next and the answer was, "I have not chosen him." In all Jesse had seven of his sons pass before Samuel.

Seeing that the seventh son was the last, and thinking that one of the seven must be chosen, Samuel may have had the horn of oil ready to pour it upon the head of this last one. However, the Lord told him again, this was not the one. Samuel's mind was filled with confusion. If this was not the one, then who was? Had the Lord sent his prophet to the wrong house?

Somewhat perplexed, Samuel asked Jesse, "Are all your children here?" Jesse might have stammered a bit as he said, "This is all, except for the youngest."

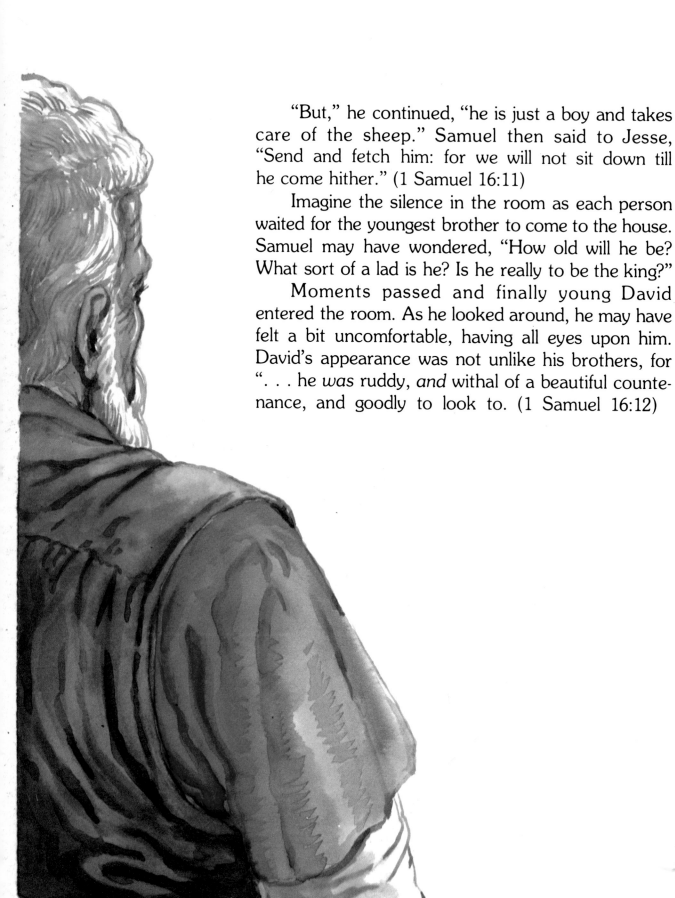

"But," he continued, "he is just a boy and takes care of the sheep." Samuel then said to Jesse, "Send and fetch him: for we will not sit down till he come hither." (1 Samuel 16:11)

Imagine the silence in the room as each person waited for the youngest brother to come to the house. Samuel may have wondered, "How old will he be? What sort of a lad is he? Is he really to be the king?"

Moments passed and finally young David entered the room. As he looked around, he may have felt a bit uncomfortable, having all eyes upon him. David's appearance was not unlike his brothers, for ". . . he *was* ruddy, *and* withal of a beautiful countenance, and goodly to look to. (1 Samuel 16:12)

As Samuel looked at this fine young man, he heard the Lord say, "Arise, anoint him: for this *is* he.

"Then Samuel took the horn of oil, and anointed him . . . and the Spirit of the LORD came upon David from that day forward. . . ." (1 Samuel 16:12, 13)

This was the beginning for David. Or was it? It is difficult to say just where things really do begin. Certainly the Lord knows everyone, no matter what age. At any rate, David's past experiences as a youth must have prepared him for the marvelous things yet to come.

THINK ABOUT IT

1. Do we sometimes judge others by their outward appearance? How can we learn to look upon the heart?
2. When we look at a situation, do we only see what appears to be happening, or do we try to see *why* it is happening as well?

THE FAITH TO WIN
1 Samuel Chapter 17

Now a story takes place that gives hope of victory to those who seem to have little chance of winning.

The word "big" is too small a word to describe a certain man who was a soldier in the Philistine army. From the bottom of his huge feet to the top of his enormous head it would take a word such as "gigantic" to do justice to this man's nine feet, nine inch (six cubits and a span) frame. His name was Goliath.

As Goliath walked back and forth in full view of the Israelite army, he roared a dare to them, bellowing, ". . . choose you a man for you, and let him come down to me. If he be able to fight with me, and to kill me, then will we be your servants: but if I prevail against him, and kill him, then shall ye be our servants, and serve us." (1 Samuel 17:8, 9)

Goliath's massive body was protected with armor and he held a spear so large that most men could not even pick it up. It is little wonder the men in Israel's army didn't answer his challenge. To go against this man would be foolish and mean certain death.

For forty days the two armies, each a bit fearful of the other, remained in their own camps. The Philistines hoped the winner could be decided by Goliath fighting a single opponent. The Israelites knew they had a chance in a large battle but no chance in a one-to-one fight with this giant.

As the suspense was building on the battlefront, David peacefully walked the last mile of his journey. He was taking some food to his brothers, who were serving in the Israelite army.

Upon his arrival at the camp, David soon heard the roaring voice of the giant. "Who is that?" he asked in astonishment. "It is the giant, Goliath," his brothers replied with fear in their voices. "What is he saying?" David asked. "Listen for yourself!" came their reply.

David did listen, and what he heard brought anger to his heart. He spoke to the men who stood by him, saying, ". . . who *is* this . . . Philistine, that he should defy the armies of the living God?" (1 Samuel 17:26)

David's brave words upset his older brother Eliab, and Eliab asked sharply, ". . . and with whom hath thou left those few sheep . . . ?" This brother thought David should go home to the sheep where he felt David belonged. But others, hearing the brave words of the lad, hurried to tell Saul. Saul then sent word for David to come to his tent. (1 Samuel 17:28)

At times David had played music on his harp for King Saul, so the two were not strangers to each other. David begged Saul for the opportunity to fight the giant, and at first Saul was amused. But as David continued pleading, Saul's expression changed. In his heart he knew David was not just an ordinary young man.

To the amazement of his advisors, the king agreed to let young David represent Israel in this battle where everything was to go to the winner.

David was fitted with Saul's brass helmet and coat of mail, but they were uncomfortable. Knowing that the only armor he needed was the armor of God, David left Saul's armor behind. After being wished good fortune by the king and others, brave young David walked forth across the lonely strip of land that separated him from the giant.

The eyes of both armies watched the two seemingly unmatched opponents gradually move closer to each other. The Philistines must have been amused as they saw this young man of ordinary stature come into full view. They probably remarked to each other, "He has no armor!" and "It must be a joke." But the Israelites knew it was no joke. Some may have thought, "Why did Saul let him go? He will lose and we will become slaves."

Goliath could not believe his eyes. After forty days of shouting he didn't expect anyone to come to battle. It is certain he never expected his opponent to be a youth without armor. He shouted words at David that sounded all the louder because the entire valley was filled with silent suspense: "*Am* I a dog, that thou comest to me. . . . I will give thy flesh unto the fowls of the air, and to the beasts of the field." (1 Samuel 17:43, 44)

David's reply must have brought a thrill to all his countrymen. He said confidently, "Thou comest to me with a sword, and with a spear, and with a shield: but I come to thee in the name of the LORD of hosts, the God of the armies of Israel. . . ." The brave young man continued and told Goliath that it would be his flesh and not David's that would be fed to the birds and beasts, adding ". . . that all the earth may know that there is a God in Israel." (1 Samuel 17:45, 46)

David had already picked up five smooth stones from a small brook he had crossed. In his hand was the sling he had often used to protect his sheep from wild beasts.

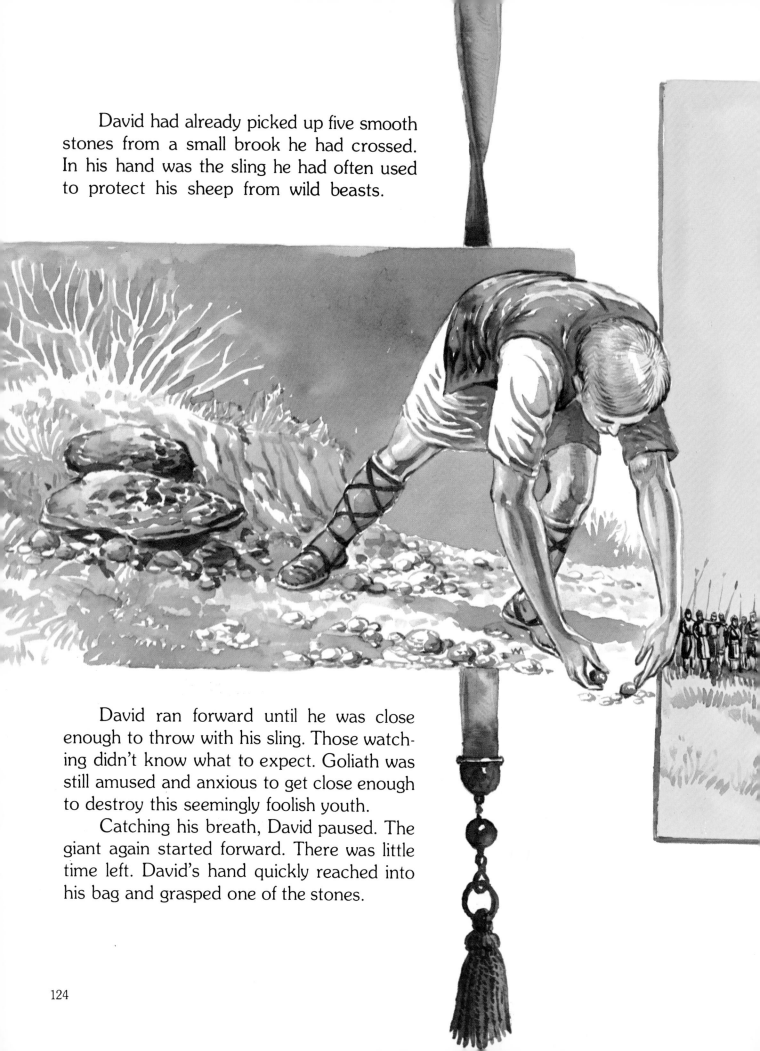

David ran forward until he was close enough to throw with his sling. Those watching didn't know what to expect. Goliath was still amused and anxious to get close enough to destroy this seemingly foolish youth.

Catching his breath, David paused. The giant again started forward. There was little time left. David's hand quickly reached into his bag and grasped one of the stones.

Putting the stone in the sling, he whirled it around and around as the giant hurried forward. All those watching could see the battle was nearly over. Even the Philistines felt sorry for David, who they thought would soon be cut in two by the mighty sword of Goliath.

But what happened? The stone flew so quickly it was hardly seen. As it struck the giant in the forehead, Goliath staggered and fell. The Philistines must have wondered, "What happened? Did he trip? Can he get up?" The Israelites, finally realizing what David had done, may have yelled, "He got him! He did it with a sling!" Then a mighty shout of victory went up in the Israelite camp.

"So David prevailed over the Philistine with a sling and with a stone, and smote the Philistine, and slew him; but *there was* no sword in the hand of David.

"Therefore David ran, and stood upon the Philistine, and took his sword, and drew it out of the sheath thereof, and slew him. . . . And when the Philistines saw their champion was dead, they fled." (1 Samuel 17: 50, 51)

The Philistines could scarcely believe their eyes. Their hero, Goliath, was dead. Fear swept through them.

In panic they hastily retreated. The Israelites, with new faith and a new hero, chased after them.

What a day for Israel and for young David! What a day for all those who at times must face a giant of one kind or another. If only everyone today would have faith such as David, who knew that with the Lord at his side, he could defeat any enemy.

THINK ABOUT IT

1. The Lord seems to have arranged for this great event in history. With all the odds against David, what do you think the Lord was trying to teach through this experience?
2. What is "the armor of God"?
3. We, like David, often face "Goliath-sized" problems. Name some of these. What did David teach us we should do about problems?

PREVIEW OF THINGS TO COME

In the next book, Volume Five, David continues to rise until he finally becomes king. Although King Saul becomes envious of the fame of David, his son Jonathan and David become loyal friends. But Saul's jealous hatred for David continues and David is forced to flee into the mountains to avoid being killed by the confused king.

After Saul is killed in battle, David becomes king and has some thrilling experiences. Then David does a wicked thing. He has a man killed just so that he can marry the man's wife.

After this event David's life becomes sad. His son Absalom, rebelling against him, tries to become king but is killed. Because David's heart is nearly broken, he seeks comfort in writing beautiful poems or psalms. Even though his life is sad, he knows that God still loves him.

After David's death we will meet a person who some people feel was the wisest man to ever have lived—David's son, King Solomon. We will learn how Solomon's wisdom came from God.

After the death of Solomon, the kingdom of Israel becomes divided and weak. The people begin to worship false gods. Then the mighty prophet Elijah is called. He spends much of his time waiting but performs some mighty acts. A great contest takes place between God and some false gods. After we have been excited by the power of this great prophet Elijah, we will bid goodbye to him as he goes to heaven in a fiery chariot.

Elijah's student and young friend, Elisha, becomes the new prophet and performs many miracles. Through the works of Elijah and Elisha Israel once again returns to the worship of the true God.

Volume Five will show us again how very much God is interested in the welfare of his people.